ELECTROCUTED

Inspiring True Story
of Faith, Courage
and the Will to Live

DENNY WASMUND

TABLE OF CONTENTS

FOREWORD

This is a true story of my life from the beginning to the day I was electrocuted by faulty equipment and literally died. I'm going to do my best to explain to you the peace I felt when I left this earth and the agonizing hell it took me through to get back to where I am today.

To: Jeanie
God bless

I WAS ELECTROCUTED

Chapter 1

GETTING STARTED

I had just graduated from high school. I was ready for the world. My mother and father relocated to Florida, so I had to move out quickly. I graduated in June and I was out of the house by August. I had a chance to go to college, but that wasn't the plan. So I went to work and rented an apartment. I didn't like the fact of renting an apartment because it didn't feel like my own, so it didn't last long. I started renting with my twin brother and a great friend that we went to school with, whose name was Chris. We all had girlfriends at the time, so having the house we rented was short-lived.

Now let me tell you how I met my future wife, Christine. I was a senior in high school and she was a sophomore. I was walking down the hallway with a buddy and I saw her at the drinking fountain. I was thinking she was the one, you know... till death do you part. What a blessing from God. It was a miracle. I still to this day remember that moment so vividly, but I'll get back to explaining that later. At this time I worked at a factory, working at the presses on the night shift. Every time I drove up to the plant I would look at the sky and wonder, How *long will I be here at this job?* I knew I didn't want to make a career of it, but my mind was set on getting settled, so I could ask Christine to marry me.

Now Christine had two years of school left. I thought she wasn't going to wait for me. Her father didn't like me much. I was older and out on my own and she was still in school. Christine's mother didn't have a problem with our relationship. Two years later, Christine graduated and started cosmetology school. It was great. She was working on being a hair stylist and a manicurist. We were young. We thought this was the plan. Christine had just a few hours to go with graduating from cosmetology school and my twin and I and our good friend were still renting the house in Rochester. Christine and I had been dating for three years. If she and I were going to live together, we were going to get married. That was my belief. We were working on buying a house of our own, so this meant another change. Breaking the news to my brother and Chris was not easy. I didn't know how they were going to react. Thank God they were happy for me, but on the other hand, they didn't want me to go. We had great times. It was an experience I will never forget.

So the time had come to ask Christine to marry me and it was amazing! The house I was renting had an upstairs, so that was where I spent most of my time. Downstairs were the other two bedrooms. One night I had made up my mind. I was very nervous. Christine and I were sitting on the sofa watching TV. Summer, our dog at the time, was lying along the side of the wall. She was just a puppy, probably trying to stay cool because it was so hot up there all the time. I'm not sure if Sunshine was there; the cat I got her for Valentine's Day.

"The time has come," I said, looking at Christine. "Sorry I'm getting emotional," as I reached for her hand and got on one knee with tears in my eyes and said, "Will you marry me?" "Oh, yes!" She said. The thought and feeling that ran through my body was amazing—a feeling I will never forget. It's amazing what Jesus can do!

At this time we were planning our wedding. We didn't give ourselves much time. As a matter of fact we planned the wedding and paid for it in about four months—I mean getting her dress, the banquet hall, the whole nine yards. The reason we planned it in such a short time is because we had just bought our first home in Clinton township. We were now married and homeowners, and everything I prayed for had come true. I finished the job at the factory because being in the factory was not for me. I was more of an outside guy, so I went into manual labor. After about a year the union saw me working at the Chrysler plant and asked me if I wanted to join the union.

Now mind you, it was about 90 degrees in the middle of summer and I was pretty fit. I was working out six days a week and also eating healthy. Joining the union was a no-brainer… they were offering me more money. So we went to a coffee shop and signed the papers. The next day I was a union guy. At this time it was 1996 and it just seemed right. Everything was great. I had security with my job and Christine as my soon-to-be wife. It couldn't get any better than this, or so I thought….

I'm sorry. Some of this is difficult to remember. I will explain later.

One thing I learned in my life is patience. I started to

work at twelve years old. I know you may think that's a little young, but not for my family. I started as a caddy at a real nice golf course, Bloomfield Hills Country Club and Great Oaks Country Club. Now when I say nice I mean doctors, lawyers, etc., so if you didn't have manners or respect for your elders you either learned quick or you weren't going to be there. Let me tell you, that was one of the best experiences of my life. From twelve to seventeen years of age it was tough. Getting dropped off at 6:00 a.m. and getting picked up at dusk wasn't easy for a twelve-year-old, but now looking back, it was one of the experiences that made me who I am today.

I got a lot from the experience of helping a doctor or lawyer sink a putt. Or giving him or her the right yardage to the hole, or giving the right club to hit the ball in a championship game or an invitational. As time went on, they could see that I was a great caddy, so they would recommend a double bag; where I would caddy for two people at the same time. That became the norm after a while. That just meant more money. I should be honest; helping out the family is what we did. My twin brother, and my older brother did the same. I didn't get to keep the money that I earned, but I always got fed and I always had clothes to wear. My father was a great man, a hard worker and that is an understatement. So sometimes I thought that was how he wanted me to be. It really taught me what I know today. My mother is a very strong person, a very loving person, a very faithful person. Growing up from the time I can remember, that person did not exist, only a few times.

Let me be very clear, my childhood along with my brothers and sister, was very difficult. I thought all of the screaming and fighting and dysfunction was normal. Until the 8th grade, when a counselor came to the class room and said, "If this is happening in your family then this is not normal." My mother is an alcoholic,and that is all I knew my whole childhood until I graduated from high school and left home. What I went through as a child and young boy happened all the time. I know I'm not any different from anybody else, but you can believe me, it made me a strong human being. I had a choice to either do the negative or to do the positive. I chose not to do those things; the drinking and smoking. I thank my mother and father for the experiences that I had to endure because that's what made me who I am today. Praise to You, Lord Jesus Christ. Now whoever is reading this, God bless you. I pray for you, and I know that if I can get through this, so can you. I didn't make it alone. Let me explain.

There was a time my older brother stayed at our house that my wife and I had bought. As my brother and I were visiting in the living room, we decided to look at my wedding video. My brother was sitting on the couch and I was sitting in my chair, we were watching the video and talking back and forth. We were laughing and crying about how everybody was dancing and how everybody was growing up so fast. All of a sudden I heard my brother say, "Turn that video back." I didn't think anything of it, but my brothers eyes were wide open like he had seen a ghost.

Now at this point in the video I was sitting in a chair, and it had something to do with the garter. Christine had to put the garter on my leg. As I was sitting there, my brother said, "Look, don't you see that?"

I said, "See what?"

"Come on its right there."

"Where?"

"On your chest! It's the silhouette of Jesus' face, right there on your chest."

I looked at this and I was amazed. It really did look like Jesus' face. We pondered this image for a period of time—we even tried to say that was not His image. Whatever we tried to do, it didn't discredit what we really saw. It's funny. We were going back and forth about whether we should tell anyone or show people the video, but it never came about, until now. Now as you read on I hope you understand how significant that period of time was in my life. My brother only stayed a few weeks and then he had gone back home. Sometimes I think that was the reason he visited, to show me how God's love is with all of us.

You may not be religious, or maybe you're at a point of your life where everything is going great. Please take my experience and know that it is in God's hands, and **not** ours.

Chapter 2

DETROIT, MICHIGAN

That's where I was born on March 25th, 1975. I'm three minutes older than my twin. He was called the bonus baby. We are fraternal twins. That was always the joke, people would say, "You guys look identical," but being fraternal we were two separate eggs. My mother, God bless her, almost lost her life having us. She lost a great deal of blood in a very short period of time. Amazingly my mother is very strong, both physically and with her faith. My mother recovered very well. My brother and I were the last of the kids. There are five of us. My brother and I were always together, we were like two peas in a pod. My mother and father would always say we had our own language; we would communicate with different sounds and understand each other. The feeling I have for my brother is very special, different from my other siblings. So you could say we have a special bond. If you're a twin and you are reading this, you know what I mean. When it came to our birthday or Christmas when there were gifts to be given, I always would think we were going to get the same thing but in a different color. It was frustrating at times. Being a twin wasn't easy. People would always ask, "Do you guys play tricks and fool people?" We weren't like that. I had different taste than my brother.

I thank the Lord every day for my twin; I didn't realize how important he would become to me later in life. My childhood wasn't the easiest though... let me explain. Being the youngest of three, my oldest brother never went easy on me. Playing football was a great example of that. Sometimes I thought he was tackling me like I was one of his enemies. I supposed I could accept that from an older brother. But he was always there if you needed him. My other brother, poor guy, was stuck in the middle. He always got the bad end of the stick. My sister was the only girl. If you're the only girl out of four boys you know what I mean, but then again we grew up in a very dysfunctional home.

My mother is an alcoholic and I didn't understand what was happening to me until the eighth grade, when a counselor came into our classroom and spoke about it, and he said, "If this is happing in your family then this is very dysfunctional and it's a big problem." It's funny that's all I remember about that moment. I thought it was normal to be spanked uncontrollably with a belt, wooden spoon, flyswatter, or a hand. For something as a simple as walking in the room the wrong way, or saying something out of order like, "I'm hungry." There would be many nights I would wake up in the middle of the night with my bedroom door open, hearing glass dishes crashing to the floor. The kitchen light would be on and the screaming of my mother was so overwhelming. I would cry so hard that it felt like my face was on fire.

We had moved to a place called Goodall's out in the country. It was a stone house that was half-finished and my father had finished the stone work later on. There was also a pond in the back. I'm not sure how much land, but there was a lot. I'll never forget the big weeping willow that was there in the yard. I still can't believe my father would drive back in forth to work in a Ford Maverick. The winters were horrible, and I don't know how he did it.

My father is a very strong man. I can remember getting up one night and walking to the kitchen, but before I could reach the kitchen I was frozen with fear to see my father on the kitchen floor on his back with my mother on top of him, clawing his chest with her long fingernails. I could see the bloody scratches on my dad's chest. I heard my mother scream at the top of her lungs, "Call the police!" to my brother and sister, while my father was saying "No!" I never could understand why my mother wanted us to call the police when she was the one beating my father.

When my mother drank, she would turn into a completely different person. That was a long night. The house was turned upside-down. Every dish was broken and all the glasses, and the dinner we never got to finish that night was all over the house. It was spaghetti that night, and it was all over the walls. You couldn't even walk through the house without cutting your feet. As a kid living in Goodall's, that's all I can remember, my mother drinking and fighting, waking up in the middle of the night screaming and crying. There's only a few times I can actually remember my mother sober.

Chapter 3

―――― ∾ ――――

GOODALL'S

I don't really remember any good days when we lived in Goodall's. The times I do remember, my mother would smile, and she always loved to put on makeup and do her hair and her nails. I'll always remember her nails. She loved painting them and putting on beautiful designs. They were always fancy-looking and long. Every once in a while she would do other people's nails. I always thought that would be great for her to do as a profession, but that never came to be. I think those were the times I remember her sober. Living there was not easy. For one thing, the winters were rough. I can remember we didn't have much heat. There was a space heater that we would use, and it was a kerosene heater. We would have it in the hallway at night and in the kitchen in the morning. I'll never forget the smell of the kerosene. That smell will stick with me for the rest of my life.

There were plenty of times I would get too close to it and burn myself. In the mornings before school my brothers and sister would eat around the table and the space heater would be right next to my brother. I would play this game to see who could make it around the top of the heater with their cornflakes on their spoon before spilling it on the heater. We always dripped on the heater. But of course we did this without getting caught by our mother, because if she caught us, it wouldn't be good. Oh, and the cornflakes? I hated them, especially when they got soggy, so I learned to eat them quickly. I was always on edge, so eating fast was normal for me. The faster I ate, the sooner I could be out of the room. That's the way I looked at it.

I was always looking and being aware of my surroundings. I had to. I just didn't know what was going to happen next. That's how I remember most of my childhood. I was always scared to look at my mother. If you looked at her a certain way and she didn't like it, you got it. I mean, I could walk past her for no reason and get backhanded in the mouth and that would start it. Don't get me wrong, I wasn't the perfect kid, but I really didn't have a choice to do wrong. Any simple mistake and I got it. Any spanking turned into a beating, and if I accidentally said a bad word, trust me, with no warning I got the soap, and it wasn't just a taste. I ate it.

I'll never forget the time my mother made my brother eat hot sauce out of the bottle to try to break him from sucking his thumb. I thought that was horrible. Seeing what my brother went through was very difficult for me, and seeing what my sister had to go through was tough, too. The bruising under my arms from my mother pinching me was always there; that's how she would get my attention. Going to school was very difficult. I didn't want the other kids to see it, but they did.

Growing up with an alcoholic wasn't easy, but I prayed and prayed that I would never end up like that. I can remember one Christmas my brother and I got three-wheelers. We would ride them in the kitchen and then into the living room—that was fun. But if there was ever a good moment, it was short-lived. That's just how it went.

Later that day I can remember my mother chasing my oldest brother into the living room, passed the Christmas tree, and into a corner. Hitting him with a broom handle. But my brother was the oldest child, and the next moment would change everything between my mother and my brother. My brother finally had enough. He took the broomstick away from my mother, broke it over his knee, and left. That night seemed like it went on forever. I was so tired of crying. My face was sore, but there was no sleeping because every time I went to shut my eyes something else would crash to the floor.

Now being the youngest, I saw a lot. I would pray all the time for the Lord to make my mother stop drinking. There was a time my brother and I were horsing around in our bedroom, back and forth, throwing our Care Bears around. Yes, I had a Care Bear. But anyway, we threw it and it hit the light on the ceiling and broke the light. All I could hear was my mother's footsteps coming down the hallway. She turned and looked into the room, and looked at the light on the floor, and went ballistic on us. Let's put it this way, the beating she gave us was so bad, that my brother never forgot the screaming we were doing, and she wouldn't stop. She would beat us so harshly that I would cry so hard I felt like throwing up, but if I did, I would get beaten even worse. That's how she spanked us when she was drinking. I don't remember the beatings. I figure I blocked them out after a while, but I'll never forget the feeling I felt. I don't think that ever goes away. At least it hasn't yet. It always felt like walking on eggshells when I was at home. There was never a dull moment.

My dad worked a lot. I would only see him in the evenings when he came home from work, but it always seemed like he was fighting with my mother. So I would try to get outside as much as possible. Now with all this anxiety and pain built up, I believed that this was normal. I can remember the kids down the road from us; it was a dirt road. We would throw rocks back and forth to see who would get hit first...it was pretty bad. We never got caught doing that, thank God. We would catch the bus every day at the end of the road. The bus stop never went well. There was always some kind of problem. That's just how it was, and we weren't too happy.

I can remember my brother missing the bus one time, and my mother walking down that long dirt road, and catching up to the bus driver. She said some words to the bus driver that no kid should ever hear, but honestly, that's not what I was worried about. I was worried about the fact that she had been drinking all day. I knew what that meant... one of us was going to get it. If you didn't get it right then, you knew you better be looking over your shoulder, cause you never knew when you were going to get it.

To see the abuse my brothers and sister had to take, even my twin brother, those moments have made me who I am today. I could have made my life a complete mess, or stayed strong and stayed on the right track, and that's what I did. Eating dinner was a very difficult thing to do, because most of the time my mother was drinking for most of the day, and there would be a lot of tension and anxiety around the table. One time we were all around the table; we did that a lot, because if there was one thing my mother did, is she made sure we ate. Now when we ate, we didn't have much to choose from. It was usually either hot dogs, mac and cheese, or spaghetti. On a rare occasion we would have pizza. I remember the fish sticks, too. There was only one time that I remember having McDonalds, and it was when we went to see our grandparents, my dad's mom and dad. They lived up north and we had to stay with them for about a year, which was very difficult.

Well, when they stopped to eat I can remember them asking me, "What would you like?" and I couldn't say anything. When they looked at me there was the strangest look on their face, like, "Have you ever had McDonalds before?"

When it came to eating at our dinner table, it was very nerve-racking and there was a lot of anxiety and tension at the table, especially when my mother was drinking. There was this one incident for example. We were all eating at the table one night and it was bean casserole, and well, I have to admit it fed all of us. But anyway, we are all sitting there on pins and needles. The table was just about to be set and we were supposed to be eating by now. We had our smiling cups out and they were yellow. I'll never forget those cups. We also had our plates in front of us, but no food on them. We were all on edge, when all of a sudden I looked up and I saw my sister take her cup, which had milk in it, to her mouth. Knowing that she was not taking a sip of the milk, I knew what she was doing. She had so much anxiety built up that she had thrown up into her cup of milk.

Now I was thinking if Mother saw what my sister had done, she would get beaten. It still took a while for the food to get to the table. So as we were sitting there not moving, the casserole was served, and what you were served, was what you ate. Don't get caught not finishing your meal, or you were going to wear it. As you can imagine, we were all sitting there trying to finish the bean casserole, and as we finished our plate and drank our milk, I had to sit there and watch my sister finish her plate and drink her milk. I still today can't believe she did that. And if you're wondering, to this day I don't eat bean casserole, cantaloupe, or peas if I don't have to.

I ate my dinners as a kid with nervousness and anxiety, with butterflies in my stomach. I just never knew what my mother was going to do, but I knew it wasn't going to be good. Not good was an understatement. We had gotten through that meal without any danger, thank God. But it was short-lived, because the next week we had spaghetti. We had a lot of spaghetti it seemed like, maybe because we had leftovers all the time. So we were all sitting there around the table, my sister and my brothers were there. I don't remember seeing my older brother. There was a lot of tension at the table that night. My mother had been drinking that day, so we were all on pins and needles. You could cut the tension with a knife. My dad wasn't around at the time.

Now at this time the spaghetti was on our dishes and we were ready to eat, and it was scorching hot. I can remember seeing the steam coming off the noodles. Out of the corner of my eye I saw my mother walking around the table where my brother was sitting. She got where he was and stood over him for a few seconds. She had asked my brother something that I can't remember, and if you didn't answer her with what she wanted to hear, things were going to be bad. The next thing that happened will stick in my mind forever. Whatever my brother had said, it wasn't the right answer, because when I looked up, all I could see was my mother taking my brother's head and pushing it right into his plate of scorching hot spaghetti. Now that pretty much just started the night off. I never did finish that meal. Most of it ended up all over the walls that night, with the dishes crashing to the floor.

I can't remember ever finishing a meal without feeling anxiety or nervousness. This is a lot of how my childhood was. Sleeping at night was always difficult too because I never knew if my mother was going to turn the house upside down. If she did I would wake up to the loud bangs and crashes to the floor, so I would tuck the sheets close to my face and pray that it was going to be okay. I had lived there in Goodall's from when I was a little baby till I was eight or nine, and then we moved back to the city. Goodall's was the stone house, the acres we had and the pond, the great oak tree we had and the play-house my dad and my uncle had built for us. It's the evil moments as a child I'll never forget, but if I hadn't gone through those moments I wouldn't be who I am today and I thank our Lord Jesus Christ for that.

Chapter 4

BACK TO THE CITY

What a change! We had to make new friends, the school was different, the whole atmosphere was different. But one thing that didn't change was the anxiety and nervousness, which was even worse. Not knowing what was going to happen next, it was different, that's for sure. I liked being out in the country. All of my friends were there. These were close friends and as soon as we moved, I never did see them again.

It took a long time to get used to the city. Apparently I had developed a sleep walking problem. The reason I say this is because of one night, in the middle of the night. The house that we moved into had an upstairs and a downstairs. My brother and I slept upstairs and there was a garage just below us. It was an attached garage that you had to walk through the house and through the garage to get outside. The driveway had white rocks all down the driveway, which would hurt your feet if you walked on them because they were really sharp. So on this particular night I had walked downstairs in the dark, through the family room, and through the garage, where there was a side door. I was outside on the white sharp rocks, barefoot in my long johns, and yes, they were white.

The neighbor would leave his truck outside on in his driveway all the time. At this time I couldn't feel anything. So just on the other side of our driveway was the main street, and there were cars that flew up and down that road, which was about ten feet away from where I was. As I got closer to the neighbor's truck, I leaned over and looked directly into the driver's side headlight, so close that my face was pushed right up against the headlight. At that moment I could feel everything. I was so scared out of my mind, wondering how I got out there, so I turned and ran as fast as I could back to my bed. Trust me, I was like lightning. God must have been looking after me that night because I easily could have walked right into the street and been hit by a car.

As days went on, my mother and father were very confused about what I was doing. So my dad started to put locks at the top of the doors so I wouldn't unlock the doors to get out. Things weren't starting off very well at this new house, and it didn't get any better. Fitting in was extremely difficult. There was this one incident where my brother and I were walking home from the bus stop, which was down the street, so we had to walk pretty far. Now before I go any farther, my parents have always taught us never to fight and in any case try to walk away if we could. Not only that, I never tried to get in trouble because I knew if I did get in trouble there was going to be hell to pay for whatever I did.

My brother and I were walking by ourselves, trying to get

home and minding our own business. It was a nice sunny warm day, but it was a bad day for me. I wasn't feeling well, and there was a kid on the bus who was bothering my twin brother. I was hoping he wasn't getting off at our stop, but he did, and yes, as we were walking he was still bothering my brother. Then he said something that didn't sit with me very well. What he said, I can't remember, but what I do remember is what happened right after he said it. I reached back and hit the kid right in the back of his head and broke my pinkie finger at the middle knuckle. The second I did that, I didn't feel anything, and if you're wondering if that kid bothered my brother again? He didn't. That was the first time I had ever put my hands on someone. I had never punched anyone before that instant.

The only thing I could feel was the fear I had when I had to walk through the front door and my mother seeing my hand the size of a softball, and I had to tell her I had hit someone. Trust me. I tried to work around it. I told her everything but that. There was one thing about my mother, you couldn't lie to her. The moment you looked at her, she could tell if you were telling the truth or if you were lying. I ended up with a cast that summer. It was awful, and I wasn't able to do much. There was this one day I came home from school. I remember it was the middle of the week. I was having a great day. School was good, and I had no anxiety or unevenness. I was feeling happy that day, though it would soon change. Walking through the front door, that would all finish with the blink of an eye.

There was my mother sitting in her chair. She had her nails done and she had her makeup done. She had a lit cigarette in her hand with a beer on the table next to her. As soon as we made eye contact I knew it was going to be a bad night. Every time I looked at my mother, that was the feeling I would get.

So as I walked by my mother, nothing happened until I got about ten feet away, and then it happened. We had a fifty-gallon fish tank that was just across from where my mother was sitting, and on the table were two rocks that my brother and I had made in school for her. The rocks had some kind of print on them, and then they had a nice clear finish on them. I can remember my dad worked hard on that fish tank, putting fish in there and cleaning the tank so it was really nice to look at.

Then my dad walked through the door. As soon as I looked over to see my dad, I saw my mother reach over to the table and pick up one of the rocks, and throw it directly into the fish tank. All fifty gallons of water and every fish was on the floor. At that moment I was frozen with fear. I couldn't move and I heard my dad say, "God damn it, Laura!" and that started the destruction of the night. Everything was soaking wet. I just stood there wondering how my dad was going to clean this one up.

After what seemed like an eternity, I turned around and jetted to my bedroom. As my dad tried to talk to my mother, she just sat there with a look, and a sense of not being there. It was very scary. That day was another rough day, but that was the norm. I would do a lot of praying and it helped. God and I had a very close relationship.

Days went by and things settled down for a while. My mother and father had gone out for a while, so my brother and I thought it would be a good idea to play with fire. For some reason we liked fire. I don't know if it was because lighters were lying around the house all the time or what. My mother and father both smoked cigarettes, so it was common to see lighters and packs of cigarettes on the tables. And yes, I tried the cigarettes at one time and found out the hard way that they weren't for me. I tried to smoke a pack and it turned me green and I was sick. It was terrible.

Now at this point we were going to set this paper on fire just to see what it was like. But as my brother was lighting the paper on fire I said, "Wait, I see Mom and Dad pulling up in the driveway!" The look on my brother's face was priceless. The paper at this time was burning pretty well and I was telling him to get rid of it. I was hoping, since we were in the bathroom that he was going to put it in the sink, but he didn't. He threw it in the waste-basket and that made it ten times worse. Now the waste basket was on fire. At this point I thought he was going to burn the bathroom down. I can't remember what happened to us that day but I can promise you this. It wasn't good.

With all the drinking that my mother was doing, I can remember her trying to quit drinking as well. Those times were a blessing, because it would be very calm. My mother would go to the twelve-step program and we tried Alateen. If you come from an alcoholic family you know what I mean. Those were very trying times, but if I can get through it I know you can too. There were two times my mother was hospitalized for her drinking. It was very difficult to be away from her, even though it was bittersweet. At this point my mother was going to be away for a while, so we had to live up north with my nana and grandpa.

Chapter 5

───◆◆◆───

FORCED TO LIVE UP NORTH

Things were getting worse, as if they could. I was just getting use to the new house and fitting in the new school. My mother wasn't doing so well. If you recall, I had mentioned that she was being hospitalized from all the drinking. That took a toll on the whole family. So my parents thought it would be best if my twin and my brother and my sister and I went to live with my grandparents up north. It was supposed to be temporary, but it ended up being around a year. My oldest brother stayed back. It was another challenge for me. Here we go again, another change, from the city back to the country, and I mean country. We were in Alpena, Michigan.

It wasn't like we were visiting. It was much different from that, because we never really visited them before. So as we drove up there, there were a lot of sad faces, and a lot of tension. It was different because my dad was our comfort and now he was going to be gone. My mother wasn't, but knowing she was getting help relieved some of the pressure. When I saw my dad leave, the feeling was overwhelming. It took about three to four hours to reach my grandparents' house. As we pulled up the driveway my brothers and sister looked at each other and we felt it was very foreign here. I didn't know what to expect. So we got out of the car and headed inside. It was a big house on the lake. It had an upstairs and a downstairs. The upstairs was a lot like the downstairs. It had a kitchen and TV and a spare bedroom, with a walk out to the lake.

So we walked downstairs and we were by the door, looking out at the lake while my dad was talking to my grandparents. By the way, this was my dad's mom and dad. After my dad had said a few words to Nana and Bumpa, he turned and looked right at us and said, "Don't make me come up here and get you guys for any reason. I want you on your best behavior."

Now we were pretty messed up as it was, so to say that... well, let's put it this way, it was a struggle. Then it sank in that we were going to be here for a while. Even though it was with family, I didn't want my dad to leave. It was very bad. The emotions that ran through my body were a feeling I'll never forget. I cried a lot. Then I hugged my dad goodbye. At that point I also felt myself get a little stronger. That was a lot. For my grandparents to take on three boys and a girl, and trust me, we weren't angels.

As time went on, the bedroom downstairs was where my brother and I stayed. There wasn't much room, so my brother and I had to share the same bed, and that was for the whole time we were there. That was miserable. Nana would always cook us something and we would eat in the downstairs kitchen. As time went on it wasn't getting any easier living there. I can remember my sister having a boyfriend. He would try to visit her without my grandparents knowing, and that was a problem. She was really testing my grandparents and they were getting fed up with her. My sister would always try to involve my brother and me in whatever she was doing, and most of the time it wasn't good.

My Bumpa was very strict and we weren't used to that. I can remember he would have us stack all the firewood for winter and my brother hated it. I think after a while he stopped doing it. I think my bumpa frowned on that, but he knew he still had my twin and me to do it. There was a pool house that my Bumpa would manage. It was pretty cool, and we could swim in the winter because it was an inside pool. That's where I learned how to dive off a diving board. I can remember my brother would do can openers off the diving board and the water would splash to the ceiling. The ceiling wasn't very high.

There was this one time we were swimming there and we met a couple of brothers there. They were hilarious. One of the kids was named Stephen. I can't remember his brother's name, but they were crazy. They loved the water, and they would fight with each other. I mean, I thought we were rough, but these guys were brutal. Not so much hitting each other, but doing weird stuff. Like this one time, Stephen made his brother so mad that his brother took this toy boat that they were playing with in the pool and peed in it, then made him drink it in front of him. That was messed up!

After a few months had gone by, I noticed my sister and my brother getting into more trouble. That was not good. I remembered what my dad had said —"Don't make me come up here and get you guys." There was this one incident that made my dad come and get my brother and my sister. My sister was trying to get her boyfriend to stay up there so they could see each other, and there was an abandoned house about a mile down the road. It was red house. I'll never forget it. My sister wanted to break in, for what reasons I'll never know. Probably for some warm place for her boyfriend to stay. So she looked at my brother and me and said, "Take that rock and throw it through that window so we can get in there."

Mind you, we did what my sister told us to do, because if we didn't, we got punched in the arm, and not just punched once. She punched us until we had knots on our arms. The rock was thrown and the window was broken. We were in. I was so scared at this point. I didn't know what was going to happen. We just broke into somebody's house and my sister had no remorse. We got out of there as quick as we could and headed back to Nana and Bumpa's house. A day or two went by and nothing came of it, until my grandparents got a phone call saying somebody broke into the house down the street. That was it. My grandparents had enough, and my dad was called and headed up to get my brother and my sister. Now the mood changed a little. I think it was less stress on my grandparents now that they had to deal with just my twin and I. Oh, if you're wondering what happened when my dad showed up, I can't really remember what he did, but I do remember thinking it would have been great to go home with him, but we couldn't, and that was awful. But that's how my childhood was. We just never knew what was going to happen.

So I was back to mixed emotions, not knowing when I was going to see my brother and sister again. My grandparents had a big hill on the side of their house. My brother and I liked to sled down that hill. It was cool, but on this day it wasn't cool. My twin and I were goofing around at the top of the hill and he said something to me that made me mad. So I pushed him down the hill without the sled and he went head first and broke his collar bone. That was a disaster. Not only did we get in trouble for that, but I also had to help him for weeks to put his coat on and off. It was funny because if we got in trouble it was different from home, because we didn't get beaten when we got in trouble.

The school that we were in was miserable and I hated the smell of the cafeteria. It was in the gym, and I can remember I hated eating in there. I was ready to go home. Every day I would pray for the day my dad would come and get me, even though living at home was horrible. I was missing the whole family bad. Thank God I had my twin brother. I never got used to living there. I would cry myself to sleep many nights and hope my dad would come and get us. My brother and I lived there for about a year before my dad came and got us. That day was the best day—what a relief to see my dad walk through the door to take us home. When I saw him, there was a change. He had lost some weight and he looked energized. It was great. But I didn't know how to take him, like when we were driving home he asked us, "Are you guys hungry? Do you want a Big Mac or something?"

Me and my twin brother trying to enjoy Easter 1987

I was so happy to see him that I wasn't hungry or full. I didn't know how to feel. I wanted to cry I was so happy, but I didn't want to show my dad any of that. My dad looked at my brother and me and said, "That will never happen again." At this point we made it home. My dad looked so different. Well, I guess a year isn't that long, but for me it felt like eternity. It was refreshing to be with my family again. I could feel that there was less tension and nervousness, but then again I didn't know how my mother was doing, and that the atmosphere of no drinking was peaceful. I was just enjoying the moment, taking it all in. I remember it was sunny and warm, and my dad was dressed in shorts and a nice pullover. He looked like someone who lived in Florida or something. To see my dad like that was different, because that was the first time I saw him like that. It was like he was starting fresh himself.

The house we had, you know, the one I was sleepwalking in? We no longer had that. There was an apartment we were in now, and yes, it was cramped, but I didn't care. I was so happy to be home, wherever that might be. My mother was still in the hospital for her drinking. It was calm for a while, but my sister was still acting out. I can remember my dad chasing after my sister and having the cops bring her home one night. That was crazy. My sister had a real rough time with my mother and her drinking, and so she would run a lot. You know, run away from home. She never wanted to be home. I saw a lot of abuse that my sister took, so I would learn very quickly what not to do. The patience was short-lived and my mother was still in the hospital. My dad had found a place to live, but he was still having problems with my sister, so he finally put her in a place called Allied Children's Village. That didn't last long, she ran from that place, too.

ELECTROCUTED

So my parents decided that the best thing for us, was to go live with my aunt and uncle, my dad's sister, for a while. Here we go again. It was cool to be around my cousins, but you know how that goes. We as a family didn't want the rest of the family to know how bad it was for us, but they knew. So now it was around Christmas time, and I'll never forget the feeling I had when they were giving us gifts. I've never got so many things. It was great, but we were not the ones to take a handout. We were just that way. All those feelings I had when I was living up north were back again. I just didn't want to live there. I just wanted to be normal. Now my cousins were seeing how dysfunctional our family was. So that just added to the misery. Thank God for my twin. I know I wouldn't have been able to get through all those moments without him. We eventually left our aunt and uncle's house and went back home, but it wasn't back to the apartment, it was once again, a different house.

Chapter 6

MY APPENDIX

We moved a lot. I never could figure out why we couldn't stay in one place for a period of time. Ever since we left Goodall's there was really no place I could call home. Troy was the next move, and we were renting this house from a lawyer who would do his lawyer business in the front room of the house. It was like a screened-in porch. My mom was home now. Nothing really had changed, or if it did I don't remember—but coming home from school and walking through the front door, I would see all the papers and books piled up, and the smell was terrible. The smell reminded me of what an old book smells like, when you open it up. It didn't help that the house was an old farm house, so it also had that smell of a farm.

So my mom was still drinking, and the only way not to see her was to be outside, and that's when I discovered the game of basketball. There was a church up the road. I always felt that the Lord was looking over me. And there was a basketball hoop in the parking lot; it had a steel chain on the rim. It was great, my brother and I would play from sunrise to sundown. That was my first love. I would dream about playing in the NBA. That was my release from everything that was bothering me. I didn't smoke, take drugs, or drink alcohol. I played basketball.

The pastor of the church was a great guy. I went to school with his son. They lived on the church grounds. The pastor would be shooting around sometimes, at least most of the time when my brother and I would want to play, so it was always The pastor against us, and he was pretty good. He never went easy on us either. I'll never forget, the pastor would always wear a gray jump suit and tennis shoes. My brother and I would play so much we would have holes in the bottoms of our shoes. When winter came, that didn't slow us down. We would shovel the snow away and keep on playing, even with gloves on! Then we would wait until our hands were completely numb and play without our gloves. I can remember our hands would be black at the end of the day, from the dirty asphalt and snow that would melt. The pastor must have thought we were nuts, but nothing was going to stop us from playing.

At one point, the pastor gave us the green light to play anytime we wanted, and we did. When we would come home from school we would walk through the door, maybe eat something quickly, then we were on the court playing. Whenever we made a shot it would make this unique sound as the ball went through the chain. It was great. I'll never forget the game we made up together. It went like this. We shot the ball from as far away as we could and tried to snap a piece of the chain to the ground. Whoever did it first got to keep part of the chain. It took all winter long, but finally it happened. It was raining that day and it was really cold. We didn't care though, playing basketball made us feel so good. Our hands were dirty from the ball being so wet.

The end of the day came and it was getting dark. We always had a rule that we couldn't leave until we each made a jump shot. So my brother took his shot and made it, all chain. It was up to me. My brother passed the ball to me and I was on the side of the rim, and I was pretty far away. The sun at this point was gone, and it was dark. I thought, *"This is it, it has to go in."* I got the ball and I decided to shoot a hook shot over my left shoulder, instead of a normal jump shot. The ball left my hand and it was on its way to the rim. We couldn't see it, but we heard the chain snap and a second later heard one of the chain links hit the ground. That was it! I finally broke the chain! That was a great feeling. I held on to the chain link for a long time, my brother and I went home, and reality set in. As I opened the front door, it was dark, and I was tired, so I turned on the TV. There wasn't much going on. All was quiet, or at least I thought it was.

A few hours passed, and I headed up to bed. I remember falling asleep, but then I woke up with a really bad stomachache. It was so bad it woke me right out of a dead sleep. So I sat there for a moment and it passed. So I just went back to sleep. As I was sleeping, I was having these really bad nightmares, with very large things in them and terrifying objects. Then I woke up again. This time I headed right for the bathroom, and I was in a lot of pain. I sat down on the toilet, hoping and praying that this pain would leave my body. I sat there for a period of time. The pain was so bad. I tried pushing, but nothing. Then I wanted to get sick, but I would just dry heave! I felt like someone was stabbing me in the guts! After a while, I got

ELECTROCUTED

so tired I would fall asleep on the toilet and then wake back up from the pain. I thought that the heat from the register would help, so I laid down next to it and tried to sleep, but the pain would just wake me up—and the nightmares.

At this point the pain had gotten so bad it took me to my knees, and now I was crawling on the floor and crying. But you know, the funny thing is I didn't want to tell my mother because I was afraid of what she was going to do to me. So I tried to last as long as I could, but this was it. I was now yelling, "There's something wrong with my stomach!" and I was crying and couldn't walk. Now my parents had woken up, and for what seemed like forever, they told me to rest on the couch. I was trying to tell them, barely able to speak, to take me to the hospital, because something was really wrong. As time went on I was barely able to move, so getting off the couch took everything I had. My dad got the car ready. We'd just had an ice storm, so everything was coated in ice and it was the middle of the night. We got into the car. I just remember telling my dad, "Hurry and get to the hospital." The road was so bad, every pothole and every sinlge bump felt like a stabbing. I remember telling my dad, "Don't hit the bumps!"

We finally got to the hospital and they wheeled me in immediately to the OR. The next day I woke up. I must have been on morphine, because I was showing them my scar to everyone who visited me, and mind you, I wasn't wearing anything. I remember the doctors saying, "You're a lucky kid. Any longer and you wouldn't have made it."

My appendix was very close to bursting inside me. It was the size of a banana, and completely black. It had been leaking all this time and that was what was making me sick. The poison was all in my body, so after I left the hospital they had me on an antibiotic for weeks to clear up the infection. It's pretty ironic that my twin brother had his taken out fifteen years later to the day! The infection cleared up after a while, and they took out the staples weeks later. I was as good as new again. I did a lot of praying that night, but that wouldn't be the last time I went under the knife.

Chapter 7

JAW SURGERY

It had been a few years now. I was about fourteen when I had my appendix out.

Now I was about sixteen or seventeen and we had moved one more time. This was our last move, and it was to Rochester Hills, a nice area with good schools. One thing my parents wanted for us was to be in a decent area with good schools. The house we were living in was in the Troy District, and honestly I didn't want to move again. All of our friends were there, and I thought that was going to be where we were going to graduate, but that wasn't the case. It actually turned out to be the best move. The new place was right next to the high school and there was a basketball hoop in the complex, so that was good. Things at home weren't changing much at this point. It was just me and my twin living there. My sister had left along with my older brothers, whom had left home years before. I believe there was less tension, but my mother was still drinking and that feeling would still linger throughout my body.

There was this neighbor down the way whom we had met. He would see us playing basketball all of the time. He'd also see us when we were walking back and forth from the basketball court and home. He stopped my brother and me one day and said, "Is there anyone coaching you guys?" He was a college coach for the Albion College basketball team. He offered to help us with different drills to perfect our game. I thought this was great. We hadn't started high school yet, so this was perfect. We were able to go to his games, and since they were college games that was pretty special. He took us under his wing, and nobody ever did that for us. The drills were much different from just dribbling and shooting. He really taught us balance and coordination. We didn't like it, but it was something we had to learn if we wanted to play in college one day. Some of the weekends we were able to go and watch the college team play and sit on the bench with them and shoot around, it was cool. He was getting us ready for high school try-outs.

Our parents didn't mind, they thought it was a good opportunity for us. My dad really didn't push me into the game, it was my getaway from all the dysfunction at the house with my mom's drinking. The fact is that the coach was teaching us at no cost and basketball camps were very expensive, so it worked out great. The summer went by quickly and it was time for high school. That was the best summer. I learned a lot. When I was in high school there were two guys who really stuck by my side, Chris Pinkerton and another friend and they loved to shoot the rock, too. Tryouts were coming up and everybody was saying, "You and your brother will have no problem making the team."

I was so nervous when tryouts came. There were a lot of kids trying out and they were all really good. The coach could pick only so many kids for the team, and the rest were going to have to try again next year. I didn't want to be that kid, and I especially didn't want to disappoint the coach who helped me all summer long. Try-outs lasted about a week, and every day kids were getting cut. The group was getting smaller and smaller. By the end of the week the coach was ready to name off his team. The coach had named off few kids, and then it happened! The next name the coach had said was Denny Wasmund. My heart sank into my stomach, and then he named off a few more. I was thinking, Oh, *great, the coach only picked one of us*, but then he said my brothers name. I was really happy because we really did play well together.

So now practice would start in a couple of weeks. We really had a great team with a lot of good players, and we had a *really* special coach. He wasn't just a basketball coach. He was a life coach. He had a big influence on my life and I'm very thankful and blessed that the Lord put him in my life. The man stood about 5 foot 5, but walked as he was 8 feet tall. He had this thing that he would do with his finger when he saw you, he would point and you knew he meant business. He always wanted to know how I was doing. He always had a smile on his face, unless you were doing something wrong—our practices would prove that. When something went wrong you heard about it, and fast. He demanded perfection.

I'll never forget the time when we had won our first five games of the season, and in the locker room, he made a speech to us. At the end of every speech, Coach would say, "Practice doesn't make perfect. Perfect practice makes perfect," and that has stuck with me even until today. So every dribble, every shot, every side move and every pass had to be perfect, and that's what we would take to our games. I'll never forget he had a tendency to make you cry when he got in your face. He would scream and his face would turn red like a stop sign, but it didn't bother me because as loud as he would scream it never compared to what I would get at home. To tell you the truth, it made me better. We had the best season the coach ever had throughout his career as a basketball coach; we went 9 and 0, a perfect season.

After that year, Coach retired from coaching. That was a real special time in my life. I hope whoever is reading this gets the opportunity to have someone like that in your life. It taught me a great lesson about life and about what was to come. That was just the beginning of my basketball experience at Rochester. After my freshman year the coaches wanted me to play varsity. That was a big jump, but I loved the challenge. I played my sophomore year and junior year, and then they found out that I lived out of the district, so they didn't let me play my senior year. It was really bad. That was the first time I ever saw my dad get mad at the school board. He even went to their meetings, but they didn't want to listen. It was horrible. It would have been nice to finish, but it wasn't meant to be.

At the end of our junior year, things took a drastic change. I had worn braces for about two years and I had a nasty under bite that needed to be fixed. That summer my brother and I had jaw surgery. There was no other option. It had to be done. It was funny because my brother and I would be the joke at the lunch table at school. My mother would pack us bologna sandwiches and I would bite into the sandwich and only get the bread, and the meat would stay in the sandwich. We also had what you would call appliances, and the horrible thing was that food always got stuck in them, and they were painful, too. There was a key that my folks would have to use to adjust the appliances every so often. So they finally took the appliances out and it was time for surgery. My brother and I did it together, so I wasn't alone.

The day came and I was wheeled into the OR, I started to pray. The doctors took my upper jaw and made a cut from one cheek to the other, and broke my jaw. Thank God I wasn't awake. It took them about six or seven hours to do the surgery. I'll never forget it. My face was black and blue and my lips were as swollen as could be. My eye was swollen shut. My brother saw me and said, "Is that what I'm gonna look like?"

Waking up was difficult. My head was wrapped on ice. That was a unique pain, I'll give you that. Being wired shut for ten weeks was no picnic either. It started with protein drinks every day, and that got old quick. Not being able to sleep was miserable, too. I had a chair in our bedroom that I slept in most of the time. I had to sleep upright because laying my head down was too painful. The only thing that got me through it all was knowing at the end I would have a great smile. I wasn't used to smiling much, so I was excited about that.

After a few weeks, I started to experiment with the menu. When you have been wired shut for six or seven weeks your taste buds start to get funny, and your brain says, "Let's put a pizza in the blender!" So I did, and yes, it tasted great. Then after that worked so well, I tried a Big Mac, and that was even better. I rotated that around and mixed in some ice cream shakes as well until the end of the ten weeks. Now by the 11th week it was time to take off the hardware. What a day! I thought this day would never come. I thought, *"Okay, I'm gonna go in there, take off the hardware, and I'm going to be able to open wide and be normal!"*

Wishful thinking, my friend... I got to the doctor's office and the doctor looked at my face and touched my jawline and said, "Everything looks great, let's take the hardware off." As soon as he was finished, he said, "How does that feel?"

I looked at him and said, "I can't open my jaw more than an inch."

The doctor said, "Oh, that's normal. It's going to take a few more days for your jaw to relax and open."

"So the fight isn't over yet." I thought. As those few days went by, my jaw was slowly opening and feeling much better, and if you're wondering, yes, it was great to be able to eat a Big Mac instead of drinking one. I thank my mother and father for doing that for me, because that was another experience in my life that taught me never to give up, because where there is pain there is peace. That struggle and fight was a great experience that set me up for the future, and yes, I was smiling all the time.

Chapter 8

KNOWING MY FAITH

I was baptized Lutheran as a baby. As a kid I never practiced my faith. But as you've been reading in the earlier chapters, I prayed a lot, not knowing what I was saying or whom I was praying to. I just felt it was right to pray, and it calmed me down. My mother and father would be yelling and throwing things, and it got me through the dark moments. My brother and I were the last ones to be at home, but now we were getting older. A lot of the smashing and throwing and turning the house upside down didn't happen as much.

My twin knew a kid a few doors down from us, and he was big on being in the church. He was a little bit older than we were, probably around seventeen. He liked to play basketball too. My brother was getting very involved with the church. He would go every week and he would come home all excited about it. One week he asked me, "You want to come to this church and see what it's all about?"

I was like, "Yeah, sure."

At this point he had been going to this church for about two years, so he was pretty serious about it. He was so serious about it that he was attending every week, and I noticed he never said one curse word. Finally, the day came to see what all the hype was about. I believe it was in the evening. When I got there and walked through the front door of the church, there my brother was, right up in the front row. There was a band on the stage, getting ready to play music. Then my brother looked at me and said, "It's about to start," and did it ever. There were some words said by the pastor, but then after that people started to run up and down the aisles! I'd never seen anything like this. Some of the people were crying and talking in different languages. It seemed that the Holy Spirit was driving them. Then before I knew it, the pastor was in front of my brother and put his hands on his forehead. The pastor then started to preach and move the Holy Spirit. Then I saw my brother move in a way that I had never seen him move before. It was like the Holy Spirit was moving him. I was definitely moved myself, so I got up from my chair and put my hands on him as well. The tears started to flow from my brother's face, it was very moving. I had never seen anything like it, and I didn't think my brother was that religious.

After all that, the service was over, and my brother told me he was reborn. That was why he wanted me there, to see and witness it. That was the only time I went back to that church. It just wasn't for me, but my brother loved it. That was a moment I'll never forget.

Years had now gone by and I was working in manual labor. Manual labor was an extremely challenging job, but I enjoyed every bit of it. I was making good money, feeling great about myself, providing for my wife, and paying the mortgage on our house. I can remember I would preach to the guys at work and they would look at me funny, as if to say, "Your faith doesn't come first, your work comes first, and material things. If I have time, then I'll go to church." That's how they would respond.

There was this one job that I was on, I had to dig alongside this building. It was actually a courtyard and they couldn't get a machine in there to dig, so I had to dig by hand. Go figure, it was a church. I was there to fix the drainage in the courtyard. I would show up every morning and wonder, *"Is this a sign? Is God trying to tell me something?"* The sun would shine and it was very hot out. I didn't mind the heat; the hotter the better. I can remember seeing the nuns walking back and forth from the courtyard to see what was going on. Then I would get this feeling that this wasn't for me, working as a laborer. But I enjoyed it and it was just what I wanted to do. The money was good and I thought there was good security. I was there for a couple of months before I ended the project. Even though I would get this overwhelming feeling that I was meant to do something else, I just kept on doing what I was doing, working as a laborer.

I was with the company for about five years, before my wife and I decided to relocate to Florida. What an experience. I transferred all my paperwork from Pontiac to Lakeland, Florida. When I saw that they had a local down there, I had no hesitation. When I got down there, there was a six-year project at a power plant, right in Fort Myers. I thought, *"this must be a blessing, being so close to where we were living."* This was the biggest job that I had ever been on, so I was really excited about it. Every trade was working on the job. Iron workers, carpenters, pipe fitters, cement workers, and us laborers. I was one of the guys that were in charge of the laborers, a foreman, if you will. There were about forty guys. The project was so big that to get around you had to have a golf cart and to communicate we had walkie-talkies.

Don't get me wrong, it was very tough working conditions. I can remember running a jackhammer for ten hours a day for weeks. We laborers had the grunt work, so the other trades could do what they had to do. It seemed we were the ones that had to start first, and to tell you the truth we were the last ones to finish the job too. After a while the other trades wanted me to switch. I can remember the guys saying, "You don't want to be a laborer for the rest of your life." You see, I already had around seven years in, and I enjoyed being a laborer, so there was no chance that I would switch trades.

Like I said, the power plant was just a few miles from where Christine and I were staying, so I was able to train after work. Even if I worked twelve hours I was still able to hit the gym. It was nice that in the winter months I didn't have to worry about putting on extra clothes because it was always warm. it would be 75 and 80 degrees at 8 or 9 o'clock at night. *"What an experience!"* I thought. *This is it, we were meant to stay here.* It even got better because they wanted me to stay after the project was over to do maintenance on the power plant. We were just in phase one and there were five phases. Each phase took at least a year or so to finish.

Christine had gotten a job at the church where my dad was working. He was able to talk to the pastor and he thought it was a great idea, so she looked after the kids in day care. At this point I was feeling like I got everything under control and I was making all the decisions. As time passed I started to get homesick, missing my brothers and my sister. We were chatting back and forth, even video chat, but it was not the same thing as physically being together. Throughout the year they would come and visit, so that was great. But it was still not enough. Christine and I were trying to settle in. We decided to try and have a baby, and that didn't take long at all. We tried for a month, and next thing you know, Austen was conceived! Now mind you, we were in Florida for only about a year, and then we were back home.

So that winter we went back home for the holidays and stayed with my mother-in-law. It was great to see her and Oma. Oh, if you don't know, "oma" is German for grandma. We had gotten there around dinner time. I was thinking, *"I will give them the good news after dinner."* Dinner was over and we headed back into the living room. The TV was on; Oma liked to watch TV. Now it was time to give them the good news, so I said, "Mom, we have some good news to tell you. We're having a baby!"

The look on my mother-in-law's face was priceless. At first I didn't know how to take her, but then she said, "Well, don't you think you guys should move back home if you're going to start a family?"

That threw me for a big loop. The thought had crossed my mind a bunch of times, but we didn't have the money to come back home. Everything I had was in Florida. The job, the place where we were living…we were pretty much settled in. After hearing that, I was really puzzled. But my mother-in-law wanted us to come back home and she was willing to pay for it, and to tell you the truth, I wanted nothing from her. That's just how prideful I was. I thought I should be the one to provide for my family, and on top of that I didn't want to be a burden to her.

After pondering that thought for a while, I took her up on her offer. I transferred my union papers back to Pontiac, and we stayed with her for a while until we were able to find another house to buy. I tried to go back to the company that I had left, but they had gone out of business. I had to rely on the local to find me a job, and don't get me wrong. They did, but it wasn't anything permanent like the power plant in Florida. One day, after a lot of praying and staying patient, I got a phone call from one of my business agents, saying, "There's a job starting in the morning, can you be there?"

I said, "What time, and where? I'll be there."

The job was with the gas company, and they needed a guy to dig holes all day, so that's what I did, spotting all the electrical for the guys that were running the machines. As time went on, the job was getting more secure and Christine and I were able to look for a house to buy. But meanwhile, Austen was coming, and quick. Before I knew it he was born, and we were still living with my mother-in-law. It was getting very hectic there, as you can imagine.

Practicing my faith was very important, and Saint Lawrence was where I was practicing. That was in Utica, and that's where Austen was baptized, and where I was converted over to Catholicism. I went through the program, and my sponsor was my brother . It was a very special time for me, with everything that was going on. I thought I had a plan, but God had the plan all along. And that's how I came to know my faith. Please. If you are struggling and you don't know where to turn, turn to your local priest, and I promise you he will show you the way. I am living proof.

Chapter 9

WARREN

Finding my faith was very important. Being a Catholic came first. I was eager to serve after the program at Saint Lawrence. Since it took only a short while, I wanted to learn more. I felt the Holy Spirit, which was very strong, but I really didn't know what it meant. So learning the Catholic religion gave me the knowledge to understand what it meant. Without going to church and listening to the truth and scripture, I would never have known. It's very much a learning experience, even now, seventeen years later. I pray for those that are lost, and as I wrote in earlier chapters, if you are lost, please contact your local priest. He will guide you in the right direction.

Jesus came to this earth to show that God is real, and that taking Him in body and blood is the very thing that will give you eternal life. I promise to you that it is not easy, and it's not supposed to be, but from my experience it's worth the fight.

Fight. That's exactly what I did. Every day I would get up, go to work, and provide for my family, thinking that this was what the Lord wanted me to do. I was very happy, strong, and confident. Christine and I really liked the new house in Warren. It was a new start, and thank God the local found me the gas company to work for.

Austen was just a baby. So Christine and I thought about it and we thought we didn't want Austen growing up alone, so why not try to have another baby? So we did, and the Lord blessed us with Ashley two years later. At first it wasn't so easy. Now before the gas company, the local was trying to put me to work, but it wasn't that easy, and here we had two babies. So I kept calling the local nonstop, but there were no secure jobs at the time, so unemployment and the side jobs were the only money coming in. I kept on paying my dues just so we had insurance, and praying that hopefully they would find me something. Now at this time unemployment had run out and I was getting very concerned because there was no money coming in, and not only that, we had a mortgage to pay.

There was this bump shop down the road and I said to myself, "This will do. I'll do anything to make this right."

So I went to see them and they said. "No problem. Start over there and use this sander, sand that van, and we'll pay you for that."

I thought, *"Great! I'll get this done and make some good cash!"* Wrong. It got to the end of the day and all he paid me was $25. I wondered what I had gotten myself into, but I never felt so desperate as I did in that moment. I had nothing but this bump shop. I was there for a little while, and I didn't want to quit because I knew if I stayed focused and had faith, there would be something better. Going home and facing Christine and the kids was very difficult, but I didn't show them how I really felt. I knew I was the provider and that's what I had to do. Swallowing my pride was something that was very difficult for me, so going downtown to get assistance and the bridge card was very challenging and very embarrassing. The hope Center was down the road as well, and that's where we would get our food. I always thought these people were very special to do what they do.

So my twin and I started to do some security work at different places. There was this one place that we would do security and it was one of the roughest places in Detroit. My brother and I were the heads of security, and the nights there were very rough. The mosh pit was the worst. I can remember one guy got caught in there and he was too little to be there, and the next thing I knew, I was grabbing him off the floor and his ankle bone was sticking out of his skin. He was so drunk he was trying to walk on it and it wouldn't hold his weight, so it would just fold over! He ended up out the back door and that was the last time I saw him. I'll never forget that time. I always prayed for those people and I always thought, *"This isn't for me"*, but having faith, I knew it wasn't permanent. I'll never forget this one guy that used to live down the road from me. His name was Mike. He would help us with the security. Mike was different. He was about 5 foot 7 and walked around with a Mohawk that had different colors, and wore baggy pants with a chain wallet. He had tattoos from his chin to his toes, and he would walk around like this with no worries. To approach him, you would have to be a little crazy, but that's not what I saw.

After getting to know Mike, I learned this guy was special. What I saw was a guy who would give you the shirt off his back if you needed it, or if you were hungry and there was nothing else to give, he would find a way to give you something, even if it meant that he would have to go without. And if you were ever in trouble he would be the first one to help you. That's just how Mike was, so it just goes to show you should never judge a book by its cover. I always saw Mike for what was inside, rather than the outside. This guy had a heart of gold. Go figure. Every time we would see each other, he would call me "Guy."

South Warren was not an easy place to live, but that didn't bother me. I liked it. I was able to talk to people and show them a smiling face and help whoever I could. Where we were living was pretty rough. Lets put it this way. You wouldn't leave your car outside, because when you woke up in the morning it would probably be gone, or broken into. We had a garage, so that wasn't an issue, or so I thought. Years later one morning I woke up and found the garage propped open about a foot. At that moment I knew somebody had broken in. What a feeling. I didn't care about the stuff, but just being violated was what made me sick. So I prayed for whoever did that and I felt better.

Being in Warren, I always thought, *"This is where the Lord wants me to be, helping others that are in need."* Even though my family was in great need ourselves. Switching from Saint Lawrence to Saint Clement was difficult, but we just couldn't afford the gas to travel from Warren to Utica. So we made the switch, and it was a true blessing. Change was something that the Lord knew I didn't like. Saint Clement was right down the road from us, so that was very nice. I remember I would go to the 8 o'clock mass on Sundays before starting at the car wash. The car wash was another job I had that was a true blessing, where I was able to work until the local found me something.

I'll never forget walking up there and seeing this kid named Mark. I said, "Are you guys looking for some help? I really need a job."

Mark said, "Come back in two weeks."

The next morning I was there at 7 in the morning, ready to dry off cars. I would never have thought that this place would be part of the reason I'm here today. It was great. I met a lot of good people. I would dry the cars as they would come out of the tunnel, and greet them at the window, with a smile on my face. Even though they might be having a horrible day, at least they would see my smile and just maybe it would cheer them up for that moment. There were a lot of cold days, so cold that I just didn't want to get up and go. But there was something inside me that would just get me to go every day. Now that I was working at the gas company I would get laid off in the winter and I was able to work at the car wash, to make ends meet. I would dry off cars for the next five to six years there. I'll never forget our time in Warren. It was very special.

Chapter 10

GAS COMPANY, SECURITY, CAR WASH

Not much changed during the twelve years that we lived in Warren.

I was working for the gas company, doing security, working at the car wash, going to the gym, and practicing my faith. You could say I was very busy, but I didn't think that way. It was hard work, but it drove me to be the best I could be. I was back on track, working all day, then coming home and going to the gym. I couldn't get enough. It was very similar to when I was hustling in Florida. Working at the power plant, and getting ready for bodybuilding shows. I look back now and I didn't realize how selfish I was really being.

The guys at work would say, "Are you crazy? You dig all day and you want to go to the gym?" They didn't realize that going to the gym made my job easier. The gym also helped when doing the security on the weekends. It was important to be fit, and having the look would help people make better decisions, even though talking out a situation was the best answer, and being physical was never the first solution. With my background, talking to someone who was very drunk was the best way to resolve a situation, and sometimes that didn't work.

I had all this going on and it felt good, chasing the dollar, that's how I would put it. Christine and I had decided a long time ago that if we were to have a family, I would do whatever it took to provide for her and the kids so she wouldn't have to work, so that's what I did. Working was what I thought I was supposed to be doing. Christine thought I wasn't home much, but I thought that's what I was supposed to be doing. So in the spring and summer I would be working for the gas company, and doing security. Then when winter came, I would work at the car wash. It was great. I could spend more time with Austen and Ashley, while making extra money at the car wash. Times were really good. I even got Austen into karate. I thought I had it all, and my life was perfect. I was in the best shape of my life, and at this point if you challenged me to do something I wouldn't even hesitate. Ashley was graduating from Our World of Fours. It was really special. Christine was at her best and feeling great as well.

It was tough. The weekends were a great time at the car wash, but on Sundays I would go to the 8 o'clock mass and then go to the car wash. That was the only way, because my faith always came first. I didn't like working on Sundays, because I thought that was the Lord's Day, but deep down I just felt that He had something different for me. If I kept my faith first, God would know when it was enough. I did that for a long while. I never thought it would all come to an end like it did. All at once. And when I say everything. I mean everything changed.

Chapter 11

———◦◦———

ELECTROCUTED

It was a beautiful sunny day. Warm. Probably around 75 degrees.

Christine and I were outside and we decided to restore our statue of Mary. The statue was looking very weathered. A lot of the paint was chipped off and the cement was showing. So I reached into the flower bed and picked her up and carried her to the sidewalk. I thought it would be easier to paint her outside, because it was so warm. We had decided to do all the landscaping that day. You know, putting down all new mulch and just getting ready for the summer. Austen was just finishing with karate he was getting his purple belt and Ashley was graduating from Our World of Fours and that night was her ceremony. I never thought the next day would change my life forever.

Night time arrived, and like any other night I said prayers

with Austen and Ashley before bed. Morning came, and I woke up like any other day. I was thirty-three years old. Christine was lying in bed still asleep. I put my clothes on, walked to the bathroom, washed my face, brushed my teeth, and went into the kitchen. Where I put on my boots and had my vitamins and water. This was my routine day in and day out. I was sitting there waiting for Greg to show up. He was my foreman, so he drove the company truck. Again, the sun was shining so bright that morning, and I felt it was going to be a great day. Here came Greg. I could hear that truck a mile away; it was that loud.

I got up from the chair and headed back to the bedroom and gave Christine a kiss, like I would do every morning, and said, "I love you and I'll see you later." We had a new laborer working with us that day. The guy I used to work with had left to go to into the service for a while. I had worked with him for about two years, so this was going to be different, having a new laborer, because we worked great together. As soon as we met, we found that we had a lot in common. He liked to go to the gym and work out like I did. So we would talk about training all day. He hated digging holes and the gas company wasn't for him, so he headed to the navy, and that was the last time we worked together.

I walked out of the house, and got into that red company truck. I couldn't believe that Greg would drive back and forth two and half hours each way every day. See, I moved gas meters for the gas company, and the contract for that year was local for me. That was the first time in eleven years that I was working so close to home. It was something special. I was feeling really blessed to be so close to home, and this contract was going to last a long time. At least that was my understanding.

ELECTROCUTED

Let me tell you a little about Greg. This was the hardest worker I've ever worked with, and we worked great together, and that doesn't happen very often, like ever. He would do all the inside work and I would do all the outside work. It was very important that we worked so well together because we would do at least five or six houses a day. That was unheard of throughout the company, but that's just how Greg was. I'll never forget the time he picked me up one morning and he was shaking uncontrollably. I said, "What's the matter, brother?" He went on to tell me that his house had caught on fire and he had to put it out with his garden hose. I couldn't believe what he was telling me, and he still was able to make it to work that day. This guy had no quit in him. I think that's why we got along so well.

So that sunny morning we had a meter to change out in Roseville, which was just a few miles from the house. The traffic was the same as any other morning; busy. But we showed up on time, and at that time I got to know our new laborer. This was the first time he had ever worked with gas. He was telling me he used to drive a truck, so this was going to be a new experience for him. So as we pulled up to the house, which actually sat back from the street, we had to park in the driveway.

We all got out of the truck, and Greg headed up to the front door to meet the customer. He was always good with people, so that made the job easier. He would explain to the customer that we were going to move the gas meter from the basement to the outside of the house. The new guy started to dig the hole up by the house to find the gas line. That always took some time to do, so I had a few minutes before I had to do my job, which was to cut the gas pipe and drill the hole for the gas meter. So I went back to the truck to call Christine. I jumped in

ELECTROCUTED

the truck and grabbed my phone, and dialed Christine. It rang for a few rings, and then Christine answered.

I said, "Hi, honey. Can you do me a favor and see how much the insurance will be for the T-bucket?"

You're probably thinking, "*What's a T-bucket?*" It was a classic car that I had, a street rod, and I needed to put insurance on it for the season.

Christine said, "Yeah, sure, no problem."

I said, "I'll call you back in ten minutes."

She said, "Okay. I love you."

"I love you too," I said. I got out of the truck and headed over to the hole. I sat down with my feet dangling inside the hole. I looked over to my left and saw the drill lying there. I went to pick it up with my left hand. And that's the last memory I have of that moment. As I picked up the drill, I felt the worst pain I had ever felt and it only lasted for about a second. The only way I can describe that feeling I felt was death, because that's exactly what happened to me. The drill electrocuted me. The electricity entered through my left pinky, traveled up my left arm and across my chest, where it stopped my heart. Then went down my right leg and out my right foot. At this point Jim had run over to the outlet and unplugged the extension cord from the wall, to stop the electricity from shocking me.

The neighbor just two doors down was getting into the shower to start her day as a paramedic. As she was getting in the shower she had heard this blood-curdling scream. A scream like someone was dying. Apparently my body ended up on the driveway next door, lifeless. The neighbor's name was Sandy, and as soon as she heard me scream she threw some clothes on and ran to my side to start CPR. Greg had already tried to give me CPR, but he got so tired he had to stop. Then Sandy started, but they couldn't get a pulse, so the fire department showed up because they had a run that cancelled at the same time, so they ran over to me. They rushed out of their truck and over to me. They cut off all my clothes and put the defibrillator to my chest and shocked my heart back. At least, that's what they told me.

As soon as I picked up that drill, I left here. The old Denny is still on that driveway, at thirty-three years old. I thank Jesus for sending Sandy and all that were there that day. Sandy had moved just after that happened to me. Which was pretty ironic since she lived in that house for twenty-five years.

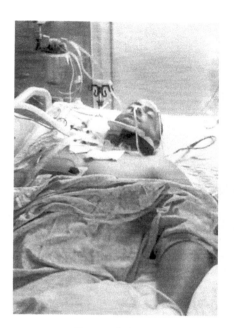

Coma 6-11-08

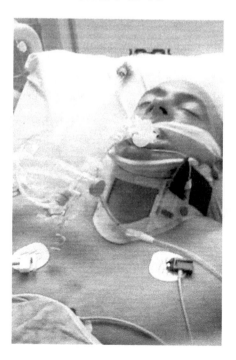

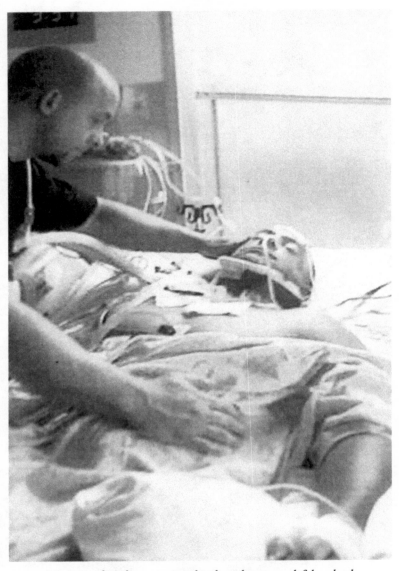

My twin brother putting his hands on my lifeless body

Chapter 12

DETROIT RECEIVING

So after all was being done by the firefighters, they still couldn't bring me back to life, the ambulance got to the house and they rushed to my side, and loaded me up on a gurney, and into the ambulance. They rushed me to a major hospital in Detroit. That was the nearest major hospital. After getting the phone call from Greg that I was in bad shape, Christine drove to the school to get Austen, who was in the first grade. Ashley was still sleeping. She was taking a nap and my mother-in-law met her at the house and they drove together to the hospital. As Christine got to the major hospital, she rushed to the front desk and shouted, "My husband is here!"

She looked over and saw my twin brother and his boss from work in the hallway. The hospital would not let my brother see me until Christine got there. After a minute or so they were able to come in the back and see me. There I was, lying on a gurney, not moving. My brother looked at me and saw that my eyes were shut and I looked lifeless. How he describes it is that he was looking at my body, but I wasn't there, and he was right. I wasn't. Then Christine and my twin went into a private room, and waited, not knowing if I was dead or alive. They heard a knock on the door and a detective walked into the room. He started to explain to Christine what had happened to me on the scene, that I was electrocuted and CPR was performed. Right after he said that, the doctors rushed into the room and said they were moving me to Detroit Medical Center, because they had a burn unit and they could treat my burns there.

Christine got in the ambulance with me and they rushed me over there. The burns that I had were my left hand and my left pinky where the electricity had entered through my palm. I also had burn marks on my back and my forehead where the electricity traveled throughout my body. They claimed that it exited through my right leg, because as I was coming out of the hole my right leg was straight in the air. The doctors rushed me back to triage to stabilize me. My sister and brother were there at the hospital. It was about 11 o'clock in the morning. I was no longer here on earth. My twin saw me in the hallway and the doctors called him over to hold my legs down while they tried to sedate me. My twin remembered that it took a bunch of guys to hold me down, and he was still looking at me and seeing that I wasn't even there.

After all that, they got me to a different room to be looked at. The doctors came down to see Christine and ask her if they could use this new procedure to bring my temperature to normal to reduce brain damage—this would take some time. Of course my wife said, "Yes, do whatever you can to save his life."

The procedure used cooling tubes with very cold water to

cool my blood down. That way, I could start to heal. Once they started that they moved me to the ICU upstairs. There were only a few beds up there, so the nurses could monitor me on the hour. I would remain in my coma for eleven days. Christine and the family had no choice but to pray and hope that I would wake up. For hours they didn't know what the doctors were doing to me. It was a mystery, living completely on faith. Then Christine and the family got the call from the doctors, saying, "You can see him now."

Christine walked into the room first, because there could be only one at a time. There I was, lifeless, only a machine and an abundance of wires keeping me alive. The doctors also cut my neck to put a breathing tube in to keep me breathing. All my family could do was pray by my side, and hope that I could hear them. Not a chance. Like I said before. As soon as I picked up that drill I left here. I went to a place that is so peaceful, that it is incomprehensible for the human brain. At this time my twin had come in to see me, but all he could do was reach across me and give me a hug, although I would never feel it. He could only hope that I did. Then that first day had passed.

The next day my parents had showed up. You see, they lived in Florida, so getting to the hospital wasn't easy. My mom was very sick, and Dad wasn't doing so well either. All they could think about was whether they were going to lose one of their children. They were able to stay close to me at the hotel downtown, so they could come and go as they pleased. There was a list that was made for certain people to visit me, but it was mainly immediate family. As my parents got settled in their hotel, my mother decided it was time to visit me. She made it to my room up in the ICU. She walked through the door and there I lay. Wires, cooling tubes, and machines going off every second. She would pray and pray by my side. After praying for some time, my mother had a vision of this long road, and in the middle of that road was Jesus sitting on this rock. He was holding me in His arms and crying. Jesus was crying because He wanted to keep me, but He knew how much I loved Christine and the kids. I'll never forget the peace that I experienced while I was gone. There was no pain. No sorrow. Only peace.

As hours passed, and then days, my white blood cells had dropped very low. So low that they had to quarantine me for a while so I didn't get an infection. The family had to wear surgical masks to see me. Pneumonia had developed in both my lungs from lying on my back for so many days. They were treating me from hour to hour. My wife would ask day after day, "Is Denny going to wake up?"

The doctors would say, "We just don't know." They told Christine that there is a part of the brain that tells your body to wake up, but that part of my brain was not functioning. They told Christine, "If he doesn't wake up, you should look into transferring him to a nursing home." They said that I only had a 1% chance of living through this, and if I did wake up I would most likely be in a vegetative state.

This was not what Christine wanted to hear. She was determined to see me wake up, and she was going to do whatever it took to see that happen. After taking all that in, Christine and my brother decided that it was time to call a priest. He came to pray over me. A couple of days had passed and there was a chapel on the lower floor where Christine and the family and even strangers would pray for me. As they were praying for me, Christine was exhausted and decided to head back up to her room that she was staying in. As she walked into the room all alone, she heard my voice say "Christine," as clear as if I were standing in the room with her. She couldn't believe it was my voice. She went out into the hallway to see if anyone was there, maybe my brother or someone, but there was nobody…just her.

Now it had been ten days. The next day Christine went back to the hospital to see how I was doing. It was early in the morning, about 7 a.m. She walked into my room, and what she saw was a miracle. My eyes were open.

Chapter 13

WAKING UP

That's when I realized I was alive. The peace was gone and the pain was right now. I mean right now. My head felt like it was being squeezed in a vice, and when I had my eyes open it was very foggy. I couldn't even make out who was who. I don't even remember seeing Christine. I couldn't move my arms or my legs. I was very confused, trying with all my might to figure out how I got here, and what had happened to me. It was very frustrating not to be able to talk, because the hospital had cut my throat to put a trach tube in, so all I could do was pray. My twin brother had brought me the face of Jesus and they put it up in front of my bed. I prayed to that image for what seemed like every second of the day, for the Lord to heal me. The days were getting very long and still very painful. I can remember one time I didn't want Christine to leave my side. Being alone was very bad.

Then the nightmares started to happen. One night I was just lying there and couldn't move. I would ask the Lord to take the pain. The nurses had me on some very strong pain meds, but this was different pain, pain that just wasn't going away. A day or so had gone by and I was so thirsty. It was the worst feeling not being able to drink. It had been about two and half weeks since I was able to drink water. The day before I was electrocuted, I was drinking out of a gallon jug all day long. I will never forget when the nurses would come into my room to check on me, every hour of the night, and walk right by my bedside, and head over to the sink to wash their hands. I would pray, *"Heavenly Father, please have them give me some water."* I would point to my mouth, as they walked by, but all they could do was give me a damp green sponge on a stick and put it to my lips. I couldn't say anything, and writing wasn't an option yet because I still couldn't move my arms. That would go on for days.

The pneumonia was still pretty bad. The nurses would have to come in and turn me, and I would have to cough it up and get rid of it, which was horrible to do. Just as I would pass out from exhaustion they would come in and do it again. Here I was still praying that the nurses would give me water. Another day went by. A nurse walked in and put a cold damp cloth over my forehead. That was the most amazing feeling, because my head always felt like it was on fire, and to have that cloth so close to my mouth. I thought if I could just grab it I would suck the water out of it, but I just had to wait.

The nightmares were getting worse. I'll never forget. It was raining very hard that night and the thunder would rock the hospital, it felt like it was shaking. The thunder was that bad. I would lay there and shake. The lightning had blown the power out and at that point I thought I was being electrocuted again. All the machines were going off, and I started to panic. The nurses came in right away to settle me down. As I woke up there was a vision that I had of a vortex in the middle of the woods, and I was running at the speed of light, everything was moving at the speed of light, but I didn't feel anything. There were these bright lights at the time, too. Family and friends would visit. It was amazing to see them all. I also felt this unconditional love for them. Not just the family and friends, but for complete strangers.

I continued to pray every moment I could, just lying there in complete pain and not being able to move. Days had gone by, and the nurses said, "We need you to try and move, Denny." Even if it was only in the bed, it was something.

Now at this point I still have my catheter in. What an experience. That wasn't the only time I had one in. They put one in when I had my appendix out too. I remember they wanted to take it out to see if I could pee on my own. Taking that out was very uncomfortable and I didn't think I could go pee on my own, so they took it out and hours went by. I couldn't go on my own. It was horrible. I tried everything. Even running hot water over me didn't work, so the nurse came back in the room and said, "We have to put it back in."

Now mind you, I still had the trach tube in my neck so I couldn't say anything, but I think the look in my eyes said everything: *You are not going to put that back inside me.* My insides were still not functioning right, so that took some time, but eventually I was able to pee on my own. That was just the beginning. I had to learn how to do everything over again. The doctors wanted to remove the trach from my neck. I was so excited about that.

Picture of Jesus my twin brother brought to the hospital

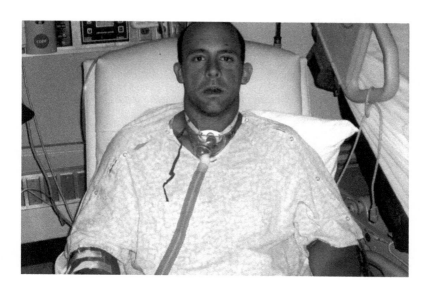

My family Austen, Denny, Christine and Ashley

So the doctors came in and said, "Denny, don't be alarmed if you can't speak right away when we take this out of your neck."

All I could think of was water. I still wasn't sure if I could say it or not, but if I could, that's what they were going to hear. So the doctor reached for my neck and slowly took out the one thing that was keeping me alive while I was in my coma. The nurse looked me dead in the eye and asked, "Can you say something, Denny?"

That took a minute or two to register in my brain, but when it did, I said, "Water."

The nurse's eyes got as big as saucers, and she had this great big smile on her face. "You sound great, Denny. I'm very surprised that you sound so clear."

The next thing I remember was drinking that water. At that point I told myself, *I'll never take water for granted again.* The nurses were so wonderful to me and I'll never forget them. At this point I was still unable to walk and my brain felt like it was on fire. But I was alive and all I could think was that I had to fight or I wasn't going to make it. Family continued to visit on a regular basis. I was just now starting to see the joy in their faces that I was alive. I just didn't have those feelings before, because they were taken from me when I got electrocuted. I would have to continue the fight in order to get those feelings back.

More time went by and the nurses wanted me to try to sit in a chair and eat something. I thought, "*That's impossible! I can barely move and they want me to get out of bed and sit in a chair?*" So I would pray for the strength and the Lord would answer. Before I knew it I was sitting in that chair and eating. My family had brought some of the trophies that I had won when I was doing bodybuilding shows in Florida and put them up in my room. Looking at them gave me more motivation.

After sitting in the chair, they wanted to see if I could walk or not. Days later, it took everything I had just to sit in that chair. *"How am I going to be able to walk?"* I thought. Taking those first few steps was great. It wasn't much, but it was something. It's funny. Just a month ago I was in the gym bench pressing 465 pounds and squatting over 600 pounds and running on the treadmill for miles, and now I couldn't even walk ten steps without wanting to pass out. Very frustrating, but on the other hand, this was something that I was going to accept. Once I was able to walk up and down the hallway, they were rushing me down stairs for rehab. I thought it was way too soon. I still felt like there was no way I was going to be able to do this. *"I can barely move and you want me to go down stairs and try to lift weights and move side to side?"* I thought. I couldn't even move my head left or right without wanting to fall over. My balance was that bad! The lights were so bright I had to wear sunglasses inside because the light felt like it was spearing my brain. There was no giving up and no turning back now, all I thought was *Forward*, and that's what I did.

I was at the hospital for about a month after I woke up. I'll never forget the smell of my room, and I'll never forget the individual who was across the hall from me. He had come in after I had woken up. He was in a very bad motorcycle accident and had brain damage. The nurses would go and see him but he would throw things at them and was very miserable. For some reason I needed to know how he was doing. I would pray for him that he would survive. The nurses didn't know if he was going to live or die. When they had me doing exercises downstairs I remember seeing him for the first time.

He survived all right, but he was on a board, and that's how they were moving him. He was paralyzed from the neck down. I never did get to talk to him, maybe one day. At that moment I remember saying to myself, *"I'll never give up, and I will get through this!"* He really inspired me. At the end of the month the nurses were trying to get me to do outpatient and move me home. I can remember thinking that they were crazy. I couldn't even walk normally. But that wasn't what they were seeing. I was thinking, *"I still have a hole in my neck and they want me to go home?"* Don't get me wrong. I wanted to go home. That's exactly where I wanted to be, but I was afraid because now I had to do this on my own. It's funny. The old Denny was gone. He left at that hole where he got electrocuted on that hot, sunny, June day. It was a miracle that I woke up eleven days later. I'm no different from anybody else. We're all miracles in some way or another. I was faced with mine and someday you might be too, and if you do, get ready to pray and fight and you too will make it. God promises that.

Chapter 14

REHAB

I made it home., but it wasn't the same. Everybody was looking at me differently now. I was disabled mentally and physically. The great thing about being home was that I was with my wife and kids. That's all that mattered to me. But everything hurt. The pain on the inside was horrible, but the fresh air of the outside was wonderful. If you've ever stayed in a hospital for a long period of time, you know how I feel. There's nothing like not being able to drink water or feel the fresh air and the sun upon your face. So being at home was very different. I needed rails by the front door to help me get in and out of the house, and in the bathroom, so I could get in and out of the shower. These were all handicapped-accessible features they had given to me. That also was mind-blowing... I never thought I would be handicapped at thirty-three years old.

The medication that I was on was unreal. For the migraines

to muscle relaxers and depression pills...you name it. I was on it. At one point my wife and I were seeing a therapist for all the issues. We would go three times a week, to try to figure why this happened to me. It was a lot on top of rehab every day. But I was determined to fight. Lying in bed and trying to sleep was close to impossible. All I would do was lie there and my mind would race at the speed of light, trying to cope with the pain. I made sure that the Jesus picture that my twin brother gave me came home with me. I hung that picture to the right of my bed and continued to pray to Him. I still had the hole in my neck. The scars on my back and forehead were healed up, but my pinky was still healing.

As time went on I wasn't getting any better. Looking in the mirror at myself was very difficult. I didn't like what I was seeing. I couldn't even make a smile. Before I got electrocuted I had no problem looking in the mirror and smiling. It was something that I did to get me going for the day. Even if I felt like crap, it seemed to work, but it was different now. That wasn't happening. Every day I would try, but nothing...not even a smirk. Depression. The definition was Denny Wasmund. Rehab was very painful. It took place at a center called R.I.M. The place had speech therapy, physical therapy, and occupational therapy, and I was doing them all.

Layren was my speech therapist. I'll never forget sitting each day in her office, trying to make sense of what I was saying and comprehend what I was reading. She was great, though, and at the end it was well worth it. Julie was my occupational therapist. She was great, too. She would push me when I really didn't want to be there. I'll never forget the talks we had about me opening a gym. The days were long and I would be sitting there putting blocks together, wondering, *"Am I ever going to get through this? Am I going to be normal again?"* She was always happy, even when I couldn't stand to be there and just wanted to be home sitting in my chair. Julie also was the one to get me to drive. My physical therapist helped me with that. Again there was a period of time where I wanted nothing to do with driving. I was terrified of being behind the wheel, but Julie was very patient with me. Now mind you, getting in the car was a whole different feeling. I remember getting in and starting the car and crying uncontrollably, and that's as far as we got that day. I also had a fear of being in the water, so we started off very slow. I was not confident at all of my body as I was before. It was the complete opposite. There were a lot of days I would cry uncontrollably to make myself drive, but just doing it was half the battle.

Our transportation were wonderful people; they would drive me to all my therapy. I can remember those cold winter days not wanting to go or move that day, but they would show up, so that gave me incentive go, and the conversations that I would have with them were very special. I would think to myself, *"Wow, they get to help people all day that really need it."* I just had a great feeling about that. Now the physical therapy I thought was the most disturbing of all, because 5 pounds was all I could lift. My body hurt so badly and it was so weak. I had a very hard time accepting that, when just a few months ago I was able to lift 65 pounds with one arm. I felt like an eighty-year-old man. I'll never forget the team at R.I.M. They had great patience with me.

Here's what a typical day looked like: Friday, September 19 2008. At 7:45 in the morning I got up, took a shower, got dressed, had breakfast and vitamins, meds and protein shake. 9:00 I put my shoes on. At 9:15 transportation would show up;

at 9:30 we arrived at rehab. 9:45 Julie and I worked on hand strength, of which I had none. 10:30 was PT with Tom for leg strength, then at 11:15 I had speech therapy with Lauren and worked on my short-term memory loss. At 12:00, transportation showed up and took me home. 1:00 lunch, then at 1:45 I would sleep—that was something that my body had to have to heal, so taking a nap every day was something I did for a long time. Then at 4:30 the kids got off the bus. At 7:30 it was time to eat something, and at 9:30 I put Austen and Ashley to bed. Lying down with them and saying their prayers was something that I'd done with them since they were born, and I was determined not to stop, no matter how bad I felt that day. At midnight I wouldn't be able to sleep, so I took meds to sleep.

This was my routine day in and day out. At first I thought, *"Is this it? Is this how my life is going to be?"* I would just keep on praying, and as days and weeks and months would pass, the therapy was getting easier. I would lie in bed at night and just cry, and

Say, "Why me, Lord? Why me? Why did this have to happen to me? My wife and kids are suffering." The tears would just run down my face. Christine would be sound asleep next to me. The nights were long, but morning would come and I knew I had to push forward. There were a lot of days when I thought I would never come out of this, but with all the help that I was given, I knew deep down that there would be an end. I just didn't know when.

Chapter 15

LAWSUIT

Winters were very long for me. I was used to working three jobs and loved it. Now I had nothing. What was given to me had been taken overnight. Looking out the window and staring at the snow was normal for me, wondering if this nightmare was ever going to end. The depression was horrible. When summer would come around I would just sit and swing in the back yard with my sunglasses on. My head still felt like it was on fire, but I knew I just had to keep on pushing myself, it seemed every second of the day, I would just sit and idle. Getting out for me was very difficult, even though going to rehab there wasn't that big of a problem. It was different. I didn't want people that I knew to see me like this. They were used to seeing the other Denny, the one with the smile on his face, who looked fit, had great energy, and was willing to help anyone. Well, that Denny didn't exist anymore, and as for smiling, that was something I just couldn't get myself to do. The depression had its grip on me, and it wasn't letting go. As far as being fit, I thought I'd never get back to where I was before I got electrocuted. As far as helping people, it just wasn't happening. That drive that I had was gone. These feelings that were dwelling inside were very different. They were paralyzing.

Thank God for Christine and the kids, and of course prayer. So as time went on it was getting better. There was no other choice. Don't get me wrong. It seemed that every day when I would go to rehab, nothing was happening. I just had to fight and have faith. The therapist that we were seeing was very helpful. It took a couple of people, but we eventually found the right one. It was a place where we could leave all our problems, which I thought was very important. I had the hardest time staying focused around the kids. I didn't want to have them see me like this. It was hard enough on them. It was.

Then the money was getting very tight. Thank God for Christine. She knew where the help was and how to get it, as far as the bridge card and food assistance. The church was a blessing, and so was the charity center. Those were places we could go and know that we would have food. My twin brother and his family would bring us food when we were low. I can remember talking around the table with tears running down my face, asking, "*Is this it? Is this how it's going to be?*" My twin would look me dead in the eye and say, "No, it's going to get better." I just couldn't believe him. There was a time when my family put on a fundraiser to raise money for the family, and that helped greatly.

In the back of my mind what always lingered was the lawsuit. That was a touchy subject when it came up in a conversation, because I just didn't know what was going to happen, so conversations were very difficult for me. That was the last thing I wanted to talk about, because the money didn't matter to me. Being alive was the most important thing to me, and getting better—the lawsuit was just in my way. I saw doctors and got different opinions on how I was doing. It seemed every doctor had a different opinion on how I was doing. One would say there's a problem, and another would say there's no problem. It was very disturbing to me.

I would think, *"I'm I really going to get what I deserve?" "And what is that?"* My brother would say, "Don't worry, it will come to an end." I just didn't know when. I would pray every day for the Lord to take it. We even went through a couple different lawyers before seeing one that helped, one would think that we would be millionaires. This would go on for a few years. It was very disturbing just because of the fact that Christine was suffering as well as the kids, and that's what hurt me the most. It just drove me to get better. I wasn't used to having something out of my control, it's like I was being tested. So among all the other things that I was going through, this lawsuit would hang over us for years. My twin would always encourage me that eventually it would come to an end, but my thoughts on that were *"Yeah, right."* But I knew deep down that God had His plan. I just had to be patient and have faith.

So if you're in similar situation, please don't get discouraged when nobody is out there for you. I've learned that first hand, and it's okay. That's why your faith and love for Jesus Christ must be strong. When it's all said and done and the day is finished, and you're lying in your bed and everybody is sound asleep, even the one you love the most is asleep next to you, all you have is you and God, and you must be able to give everything to Him. He will take it, I promise. He did it for me.

I'm living proof.

The lawsuit did eventually come to an end. There wasn't much to it, really. The laws in Michigan are different and going to trial wasn't going to happen. The day did come when I got the phone call to meet with the judge. It was an unbelievable feeling that was lifted from me. It was like the Lord had lifted a million pounds off my shoulders, and when I looked at my wife there was this relief on her face. It was amazing. The Lord answered our prayers, and in His time, not mine. $118,000 was the total that I was awarded. I can imagine what you're thinking, *"$118,000 for dying and coming back to life? This guy got screwed!"* But the money wasn't the issue, and the most important thing was that Christine was happy, and when I looked into her eyes I knew she was, and that's all I needed. Remember, it's **God's** plan, not ours.

Chapter 16

───※───

MY DAYS ARE MUCH BRIGHTER

There's not a day that goes by that I don't think about the day I was electrocuted. All of my prayers have been answered. All the hard work has paid off. Patience was something that I had learned early in my life, and I know if I hadn't learned it I would've never made it. Prayer works, it really does, but always remember it's never in our time, but in the Lord's time. Even with all that happened to me as a child. All the anger and anxiety and nerves. All of that was getting me ready for what was to come later in my life. It made me strong, but in a good way, because of all the praying that I learned to do. I never felt so close to Jesus, as when I was lying in that hospital bed. When I woke up and experienced the pain that I was feeling, the first thing was to pray, and letting everything go and letting the

Lord take it. Absolutely awesome! He never stopped healing me. He could have easily taken me home, but he knew how much I loved my family, so He sent me back. I thank the Lord every day for doing that.

Sure, this world isn't easy, and it wasn't meant to be. That's why having your faith is very important, for when the Lord will test you. When I let the Lord in fully, that's when I was free. Please don't get me wrong. I did have to meet Him half-way. Writing this book was not just for me, but for all those people that are struggling with something. Miracles are very real, and after coming back, I do feel that the Lord wants me to tell everyone that they are possible. Today I'm feeling better than I've ever felt. The Lord has blessed my family with two new additions. Their names are Emma Faith and Ruby Mae and they are true angels from heaven The Lord always makes a positive out of a negative. I would never have written this book if I hadn't been electrocuted. Even the worst thing imaginable, dying and then coming back to life can be a blessing. Please don't take this life for granted. My days are much brighter, now that I'm able to tell everyone that I'm a miracle.

ACKNOWLEDGMENTS

First and foremost I would like to thank the Almighty God for sending me back, and giving me the strength and courage to write this book.

Also I would like to express my gratitude to the many people who saw me through this book and to all those who provided support: my wife Christine, my son Austen and daughters Ashley, Emma, and Ruby, and my mom and dad and siblings. Last but not least, Greg Horton, thank you for saving my life on that day June 11, 2008. I will be forever grateful. Please forgive me for all those who have been with me over the course of the years and whose names I have failed to mention.

A special thanks to team Holy Spirit, Greg and Lori Hetzer—another miracle happened on that day two years ago when we talked about doing this book. You and your family are the true champions. I will be forever grateful. God bless!

CPSIA information can be obtained
at www.ICGtesting.com
Printed in the USA
BVHW071712080821
613692BV00001B/117

9 780578 185194